FELLOW ODD FELLOW

Fellow Odd Fellow

Poems by Steven Riel

Copyright © Steven Riel 2013

No part of this book may be used or performed without written consent from the author, if living, except for critical articles or reviews.

Riel, Steven
1st edition.

ISBN: 978-0-9855292-3-9
Library of Congress Control Number: 2013942076

Interior Layout by Lea C. Deschenes
Cover Design by Dorinda Wegener
Cover Art by Jim Jackson
Editing by Tayve Neese

Printed in Tennessee, USA
Trio House Press, Inc.
Fernandina Beach, FL
Ponte Vedra Beach, FL

To contact the author, send an email to submissions@triohousepress.org

*In Memory of
Joseph Homer Jolly
1912-1991*

and

*Harry Leon Jolly
1914-2002*

Fellow Odd Fellow

I.

3	Crayola Cruella
5	Chris Evert
7	Lena Horne
10	My Invisible Dress
12	The Teacup I Desire
14	Fingernails

II.

19	Blackberrying
20	Lost Soul
22	Upon Reading Tennessee Williams' Obituaries
27	Outside a Jar
28	For Patrick, My New Nurse
29	Meditations on Yellow
31	Sighted during a Whale Watch

III.

35	Desperate Measures
37	Walking Underwater
40	House Guest with AIDS
41	The Ferry of Your Dementia

43	Deathwatch
44	What Remains
45	After the Appointment with the Photographer Is Made

IV.

49	Weeds of Woe
51	Just Before
53	Robert Goulet Is Dead!
55	My Perfect Confession
57	White Diamonds
58	Kitty Carlisle Is Dead!
60	Postcard from P-Town
61	Hello Dolly
63	Ishmael's Afterthoughts
65	Walking behind Tennyson at Cauteretz

V.

69	Cyndi Lauper
70	Hearth Hold
72	Ophelia Approaches
73	With Nothing New
74	Swimming the Contoocook
77	Backward Glance

| 79 | Notes |
| 81 | Acknowledgements |

I.

...the face I saw in the looking-glass back of that bar, when I looked up from my glass of whiskey that evening, wasn't my own face at all but the face of a woman.

—Sherwood Anderson, "The Man Who Became a Woman"

Crayola Cruella

I came of age during one of those crafty
seven-year pauses Disney places between releases,
but didn't need the movie to sweep me away,
or even its trailer to tease me.
All it took was a cheap coloring book,
typical spin-off Hollywood cranks out
to puff profits, displayed to catch
the doe-eye of a soft-spoken boy
who would wend down dime-store aisles.
Once I had my prize safely home,
its newsprint pages lying soft beneath my palm,
I grasped the reason for that
white crayon in every pack
as I waxed in her opposing hair-slash,
highlighted its shock of black.

Instead of a broom, Cruella had glamour—
the nasty kind. The base
of her phone cradled its handset with claws;
pink cigarettes spat smoke
at the tip of her swank holder;
her jade alligator lighter
blazed red eyes each time it was stoked;
& she had a checkbook;
& she had Hell Hall;
& she had thieves at her beck & call—

so I silvered slit-eyes
of her purring Panther coupe,
blackened in points of ermine tails,
darkened peach within concave curves
of her skeletal cheekbones & shins—

my boy-eyes in a town too tiny for a drive-in,
mind's eye open, a ready pond
reflecting livid lightning bolts
or a coloring book's surging sketches—
Imbeciles, get to the crossroads!
Head off those puppies! I'd shriek,
unleashing the cackle within.

Chris Evert

"I just can't understand the attraction."
—my husband

It was how much she cared
that captivated me: the crosshairs
in her cross-eyed stare,
tracking the grass-stained ball
down to the second it met
the wallop of her racquet's face.
The whirring lenses from *Time* & *Life*,
the gallery's bloodthirsty buzz,
her first menstrual day—all this
she ruled out of her mind
long enough to smack the ball
at the shins of net-rushing foes.
Squelching a grin,
she saved six match points,
the ball a fat balloon
she couldn't miss. The cheers got meaner,
puncturing even the pluck of that tomboy
Lesley Hunt, who sobbed.

Chris's inside-out passes
proved Euclidian theorems
this seventh-grade sissy could only applaud.
Her slithering sidespin & pin-point lobs
became clippings in my scrapbook;
precise with my Lucite protractor,
I'd underline her press—captions & columns—
all I began to trust: how she squared
her palm on the grip's octagon
before each serve,

how she'd ribbon her ponytail
just so. If someone beat her up,
the world would know.

One piece of close-knit lace
sewn into her neckline's V
at Wimbledon
fastened my adoration: clad in
half a wedding dress
set off by pearl earrings matching
the cream sunshine of June,
wrong-footing Goolagong
without breaking a sweat,
she was the perfect avenger,
a paper doll whose life had tabs
my scissors could trace.
After school, I'd try her on,
let her overlay
what was wrong.

Lena Horne

i. She Watches Herself: 1960

I knocked back two martinis before
flipping on the set to catch myself.
These are the openings I've smoldered for.
Now that I've wedged my Viviered toe
back inside the sound-stage door,
the drop-dead half of a duet with Frank,
Dixieland's shears can't snip me out.
Today's houses have antennas.
MGM kept me out of the story
so the plot would splice nice if I were gone.
I have cause to dwell on it.
Sure, I would have stuck
in Tuscaloosa's craw. My Grandmother Horne
was the bastard of a gray-eyed Calhoun.
I'm not girl enough to think my curv-
aceous strut on tonight's ABC
will save the balls of my brothers
backed into some mud-rutted hollow, but
it's being broadcast from Newark to Yalobusha,
& I'm digging my Hope Diamond grin
'cause I'm about to let 'em have it
with just how smooth this "Negress"
in a thousand-dollar spangle can swing.

ii. I Watch You: 2005

Clicking past public TV,
I arrow back till I marvel, face to face
with—Who's *she?* At first I see only the sparkle
of fitted obsidian gown: mermaid at midnight.
Then you open your piano-wide mouth into yawning

indifference, curl a lip
around a lament, scorch an ex
with a blaze in the onyx of your eyes.
The only humans I've encountered
this aquiver with drama
are drag queens, who glue themselves together
follicle by mannerism by phrase.
They strive to disappear
as they reveal a diva.
My stare is stuck
to every quirky nod & glare
as you mix sadness & seduction
like gasoline & fire, cooing, coaxing,
Don't you wanna forget someone, too?
while Sinatra, overdue for a vacation,
goes through the motions,
abstractedly snapping his fingers
next to a live one.

iii. Song Stylist

Days later, biographies
fanned like feathers on my bed,
I'm puzzling out your sorrows,
trying on their contours.
They say people paid to see you,
not to hear you sing.
But your half of this duet I gawked at
aired eons after your debut
as jailbait at the Cotton Club.
By the Sixties, you'd been blacklisted,
breathed freedom in France,
left off leaning against pedestals,
crooning in a vacant vibrato
to no one in particular—

tutored by your new husband, now
each word came flavored, drenched
in style. Was this success,
or a thick after-dinner drink
for those smoky clubs in Vegas?
In my mirror, I'm
overlaying the outlines,
asking me asking you asking me:
Who sang instead of us?
What were we expecting:
revolution? Was it too late;
had the damage been done;
did just another act
upstage the song?

My Invisible Dress

> *"beads: the inner awareness of being gay. Beads represent an imaginary string of pearls worn by all homosexual men."*
> —Gay Talk: A (Sometimes Outrageous) Dictionary of Gay Slang

No one beats me up
thanks to my invisible dress.
I can strut down any street,
under the noses of
sprawled construction workers
chewing pastrami in the shade,
& can smile fearlessly
& (I hope) fetchingly
so long as I don't sashay.

Sometimes, right in front of them,
a breeze lifts my ever present skirt
à la Marilyn Monroe,
but no, no, no,
I won't be pegged by any one
look, any one straitjacket
identity. If I need a change of
style, instantaneously
my frock can be cinched or bubbled
or split to the knee;
it can be beaded with swirls of teardrop pearls
(how I'd droop under the weight of it
by four o'clock tea);
it can be brocade, organdy,
or trim, tailored tweed—
a tweed driving suit, perhaps
—with tawny gloves to match?

(I don't go in much for slacks:
they're not girlish enough for me.)

My ensembles are so easy to come by.
Let my thimble languish.
Let my steam iron freeze.
Let my savings bear interest—
I'm too busy changing outfits
to have them pricily dry-cleaned.
Unlike Cruella, I've no call
to tear along back roads in endless quest
for material.

I need not
pad my pecs,
pluck my brows,
shave everything,
shave it again,
feel cloyed by hose
on a close afternoon.

Why, in the name of all that is
elegantly simple
should I wear a real gown?
It might clash with my beads.
I'm a man
with a strapless imagination
whose armoires are endless
& hold all that he might need.

The Teacup I Desire

The pattern of teacup I desire
depicts bouquets of mauve roses
tied together by just-picked violets.
Once tea's poured out, a sipping
striptease could reveal thorn
by thorn, as Earl Grey eases
down the length of stem,
at last unveiling unopened buds,
their inviting scents
glazed beneath sugar sediments.

To lift this flowery
vessel in my hands,
to walk it to the cashier, & blushing
or not, to state, *I'd like this*,
would draw a noticeable dot
out where it could be
connected.

        If I begin to collect
teacups (not to mention matching
tea trays, sugar bowls, creamers),
ownership might imply the swan-like
curve in this cup's handle
replicates a sway in my soul,
how I'd arch my arms out of
a thin sweater if I were a starlet
at some Hollywood supper—but naturally
the indelible dots would have proliferated by then,
cups & cups & cups' worth: upside-down tulip skirts
fit for Marie Antoinette & *moi*,

angle-handled Art Decos
in lozenge-like crackle
leaning forward to chat at a café—

Might this step towards
one schoolmarmish cup unlatch all
the knickknacks that polka-dot my mind:
salt & pepper sets of every bent & hue
dishing each other across what-not shelves
lining stairs that spiral turret-high
in my dreams—grasshopper-motif bric-à-brac,
amber brooches, blue Nancy Drews,
buttons like peppermints, scroll-handled keys…

An obedient boy, forbidden his own stuffed animal,
sits on the edge of his sister's bed
when he finds himself alone. Eventually
his sweaty palm pets not the velvet,
but the shadow of her dog—

yes—honeybee heads for the rose it wants,
shoves proboscis into clenched blossoms,
rubs hairy forelegs into pollen
to pack its perfect honeycomb. The gold
splash on my teacup's handle
mirrors me back as a small dot
that's now part of its pattern.

Fingernails

      Each day I fail to trim their advance
    past where a real guy would have
bit them to the quick,
    & their tips nip my fists,
        thumbs & fingers stretch & flex,
          butterflies arching toward
            bangles of sky.

Then danger rises, rises:
   when bulbs sprout wings;
     when pronouns flit through branches
      & wrists take their first flutter;
     when the actor, all antennae,
     blends into the role
    that is his birthright;
     when he finds himself
      with O for a mouth
       needing new words.

What if he ends up a murderess?
   What if all she unfurls
     can't be folded up & put away?

      (The Halloween I wore press-on nails,
     my best friend cooed,
        You've never looked so radiant.

>   Defiant, we tottered across
>   Manhattan in heels,
>   sprayed by scattershot jeers
>   from knots of toughs.
>
>   Near some curb
>   the glow got lost.)

Week after week,
I clip back my latest millimeters,
flush their ten thin strips down the john,
prune perennials before any ruffles uncurl,

slice off powdery wings
for fear of where I might alight,
never, never letting that What, that Me
     unclench

until what I have become
becomes but this:
no not ever
     a flower taking flight.

II.

BUT IS THIS GLASS ONESIDED? asks a new voice.
—James Merrill, *The Changing Light at Sandover*

Give us today the manna of every day,
for without it, in this harsh desert we
go backward, straining forward as we may.
—Dante Alighieri, *Purgatorio*

Blackberrying

Scrunch on your back under branches
to plunder the hard-to-reach pulp.

Succumb to the pull of plump clusters,
their underslung, dusky abundance.

Then: blush as you dream lips
brushed by a lush mustache.

When a fuzzy leaf nuzzles your cheek,
you're a gurgling tot, a suckling glutton. O,

how to slurp up all this beckoning &
not get stuck, a drunk beneath a thorn bush?

Lost Soul

i.

Where men park for hours in the dark,
waiting for yet another sedan
to sidle up. One pickup
departs. The whole lot
erupts in ignitions,
three-point turns for coveted spots
            then feigns idling
(a flock of crows with the sound turned off,
rearranging shiny wings
after the never-ending
squabble for roosts).

Rear- & side-view glances.
Fistfuls of spit.
Pubis pistons thrust steering-wheel high.
Slow-motion strolls along the lips
of lowered windows. Pilgrims, looking for.

Two white faces emerge from one night.
You look like a lost soul, says one.
And why are you here, Mr. High-&-Mighty?
thinks the other, retreating from symmetrical
oil-rings reflecting off asphalt.

ii.

Mission church's white stucco defies desert,
but the side-chapel's cluttered with burned-out votives
& charred match-heads snuffed in buckets of sand.
High-&-Mighty kneels down.
In this emergency room: whispers, if at all.

Grammar-school photos
propped against Our Lady's plaster feet.
A still-life of letters, handwritten pleas
dodging intercession's triage
into Dear Heavenly Father's inbox.
Canes, crutches, artificial legs
lean, witnesses against the railing.

In the wide surrounding valley,
saguaros spread slick mauve blossoms.

Tile cools the sanctuary,
makes midday bearable. Half an hour
in the front pew, his thumbs crossed
like altar boys', High-&-Mighty stares
at the mural's zinc-flecked blues,
crucifixion depicted near the river
where conquistador corralled Pima Alta.
On edge in this peaceful gloom,
High-&-Mighty wants to sift out
what once shone. A squat woman
in flip-flops glides out of nowhere,
folds inside his palm a white rosary,
its beads like baby teeth,
its mass-produced coil
a question he'll zip
within black recesses of his carry-on.

Upon Reading Tennessee Williams' Obituaries

> *"Deliberate cruelty is not forgivable…it is the one thing of which I have never, never been guilty."*
> —Blanche DuBois, in *A Streetcar Named Desire*

i.

So, you were "an avowed homosexual."
Sin you did. Dared to make a brazen shrine of it: *I*
hope to die in my sleep…
in the beautiful big brass bed…
associated with so much love
and Merlo—

ii.

Blanche had no use for facts.
Neither do playwrights, but in the end,
you penned The End, where blared
at least some truths: four snapshots in your *Memoirs*
of Frankie "The Horse" Merlo.
What appalls one audience arouses another.
Even two Pulitzers might not outshine
a steed with thoroughbred haunches
in a skin-tight bathing suit,
giving you a cloudless grin at the beach
when you drawled, *Now, smile!*

iii.

Your Hercules squatted before you
at the sea's edge, drawing something silly
in the sand. Soft strongman
one Freudian prescribed ditching.
You tossed out that shrink instead
(backdrop: electroshock
for your sister, electroshock
for inverts, your sister's lobotomy).
Later you discarded Frankie.

iv.

Tennessee, I need to talk with you,
to face your hung-over glare,
then parry glib jabs & roundhouse retorts.
I bet you'll nail my sins against a spattered wall,
or curl like a pup & plea-bargain
to trip up my lockstep.
We both know the comfort
of typing out judgments
of another fool's pratfalls,
of marshaling rhetoric's blindered march,
carriage return by carriage return,
down an undefended page.
Of leaving our blunders in shadow,
though short runs humbled you in midday Manhattan,
as letter after letter came down from marquees.

Forgive & be proud of me
for what I must do. Brandish a spotlight.

v.

Your soft strongman you unloaded later...
                    Actually
he never denied himself to me
but he created an atmosphere
with which I, with my fierce pride,
could not very often compromise.

Stanley wouldn't let Blanche pass
without a once-over.
You set that scene up, remember?
Don't pretend to be unhinged
by interrogation: *Actually*
he never denied himself to me
            (you never gave yourself to him, huh?)
but he created an atmosphere
            (I know perfectly well what the likes of you
            hide behind your gauzy atmospheres!
            Blanche draping scarves over sharp lights...)
with which I, with my fierce pride
            (Like you got anythin' to be proud of,
                fresh out of a pig-sty!)
could not very often compromise.

vi.

That was the easy part. Let's call it Act One.
The conscience, casting stones at a mirror.
Who gets to land punches in this bout?
The jilted? The beer-slurping brother-in-law?
Or should our own echoes damn us?

I am taking down addresses for reference
when Frank goes home for Xmas.

            If I never kiss them it doesn't count.

I'd like to live a simple life with epic fornication.

    I wasn't planning to screw up again, but
    the Brit stood near the pier's end, flexing it.

One gets tired of begging for crumbs under the table.

    I never meant to hurt him.
    Yet we do it again & again.

vii.

So you nightly came to compromise with
a coaster sopped with Scotch.
Worn-out baggies full of pick-me-ups
& quiet-me-downs.

Damn your grunting humpings
in the room right off the party
—your poetic blond knockouts
he couldn't help hear about!

  …as the motor started,
Frankie ran down from the porch.
"Are you going to leave me without
shaking hands? After fourteen years together?"
I shook hands   with him.

viii.

Doses of cobalt thinned Frankie's stallion frame
to a sparrow's wish-
bone.

You took him in   near the end:
in one apartment   but always apart,
you   tucked in the other bedroom with the blond—

During the night my sleep would be broken
by the fits of coughing, loud through the wall…
I didn't dare to call him.

ix.

When *you* died, Tennessee, catty critics grinned,
couching insinuations in AP style,
joining your detractors by quoting them.
It wouldn't have surprised you: even Stella was guilty
of sticking to a version of Stanley (& Blanche)
that flattered herself. You knew how
the others ran down a leading lady's
every miscue once she left the stage,
the cruelty they railed against, but could never resist.

x.

Rose-tinted light fades in. Act Three.
A pair of men turn to each other, scriptless.
Shards of a two-way mirror
trace the truce line between them:

When the surgeon saw cancer too close to Frankie's heart,
he stitched him up and didn't say squat.
> After that, how could you look your Horse in the eye?
> Who knows better than *belles* like us
> when we're surrounded by lies?

Nothing is asked past our measure—
> When you wrote that, my dear, you were on Mars.
> Let's admit—no: avow: much more is asked,
> & only rarely could we answer.

Outside a Jar

Your kindness jars me
over the edge. Suspended on a shelf,
my lid screwed tight, my fragility was kept
preserved & sealed. You take me
down, run me under warm water to ease me
open for good, & savor my fruits.

As your lips explore me, I discover
my skin. Ripe flesh stretches taut
against my stone as your spiraling
undoes me in one continuous peel.
Your fingers forever blend my syrup & spice,
delighting in the beating & the creamy froth.

Then I recall what Mémère deemed should be
kept closed is now outside the glass. Flushed
pulp cannot last the winter in this cellar
damp. I am chilled when I understand your lips
hide teeth. And if you drop me,
my dreams of all we'll become together—
a tree, maybe a flowering orchard—
will be mopped up with the shards.
Fear nearly freezes me
when I sense even you tremble

now. Gently, you raise me
to your lips & lick the spoon.

For Patrick, My New Nurse

who led me inside the bathroom,
threaded my arm & two of its tubes
through the wrong armhole of a second
johnny when I confessed my worry
about mooning random passersby;
who planted his thighs a thumb's
length from mine to tie soft
cotton snug against skin
stretched over scapula guarding that
hollow where prehistoric wishbone soared
like prayer;
              who remained, unruffled—
I focused on the telling little
muscles at ease around his eyes—
when my hard-on rose in thanks, alive

Meditations on Yellow

i.

A frowzy blaze of forsythia:
scrawled alephs aflame,
hint of a hatchway torched open,
a fiery blink each spring
                          once stone is rolled
    from the entrance to
winter's tomb.

ii.

Honest at last, propose
a grown-up season playing Candy Land
so you can be Yellow.
Hope the card you draw
sends you to a yellow square
to emphasize you've aligned
Where with What you wanted to be.

iii.

Easter's raiment almost too rich
to be deserved: a surfeit
of yellows snug in the grass:
fuzzy chicks, ducklings,
pale eggs, and peeps—
this sweet overwhelming,

iv.

its nested pledge
defenseless against late
blizzards and crows,
when all but one plucked feather
goes black.

v.

—A lifetime's passion
for detailing suffering
in minute exactitude—
couldn't the same be done
for joy?
        Where to begin?
A '57 Plymouth's yellow fins?

vi.

Even if yellow were the color of forgiveness,
could we ever honestly
forgive ourselves? *Keep walking*
toward the light,
one self-help guidebook says.

vii.

A calculated abundance of shine
gets shot through stage-set windows,
brushes a cornucopia with a buttery cast
so Pepperidge Farm can remember.

No, Madison Avenue,
though you use what's most dear
as coinage to seduce,
I won't let you prostitute
the power of light.

Sighted during a Whale Watch

To commune with late afternoon's muted light,
to swathe myself in swirls of solitude,
I turn from those aiming cell phones
at pierced noses and hennaed roots.
My grip loose around portside railing,
I'm a cave open toward uncluttered
ocean.

August breeze and lukewarm spray
soothe even my readily goose-bumped flesh.
The wounded creature I've become
unclenches, sways with the hull's lullaby.
With windbreaker unzipped, I stand becalmed,
adrift.

Massed clouds divide. Sunlight sprints
across napping waves, spreads across my brow,
as if laying outstretched palms
tender against my temples.
For sixteen years, I never imagined,
couldn't have expected nor prepared for
my dead brother's palpable
presence.

Unbidden, warm salt streams
down creek-bed creases in my face
as if a switch were thrown
offstage

and all glistens within one membrane:
brine-tangy air, trembling sea, fireball low in the firmament
transmitting this gentle sheet of sheen—
something free of his personality.
It feels

open, angelic. Even after cumulous
bulges back across the blazing gap,
I linger over the vast, now-pearly bay,
not wanting to step away from that near
caress.

Someone else could call it an ordinary excursion—
just more whales than usual bless us with tail-flips
as they herd krill toward one spot.
We applaud and tip the salty captain.
And yes, a similar shaft of light, overdone in oils
and framed in some knickknack shop, can be bought,
or witnessed when Yahweh's voice booms
in an Old Testament film staring Heston,
but when

that wedge of light arrowed across,
what my skin and eyes at once recognized
marks these years without: before and after.
I don't know whether he'll visit
again.

III.

*That first summer I lay on the grass above it as if it were
a narrow bed, just my size, and—
lying on the ground above my brother's body like a log
floating on lake water above its own shadow.*
—Marie Howe, "The Grave"

Desperate Measures

If we played queens—Elizabeth R;
Mary, Queen of Scots—I'd behead you.
On our family's Stratego board, my indiscernible
Maginot Line would blow
your dull-witted generals
to smithereens. Even flitting
badminton could turn nasty:
well-aimed smashes raised welts,
& drop-dead dropshots
became yet more ways to stud my fuselage
with victories over you, brother,
the only outgunned opponent in sight.

At school, shame strafed me in slow motion
as I slumped with the standbys
whenever captains picked teams.
I'd taxi grounded fury, clumsy wings
to the outfield, twist my propeller
till I was a taut, knotted rubber band,
then dive-bomb you later that night.

Wolfe outflanked Montcalm's height
one dawn, captured the Plains of Abraham,
but grapeshot leveled them both.
I did my homework. I knew the stakes
grown men wagered & only sometimes won.
I played with a stacked deck: keeping
the balance of power always in my favor,
you pinned down under constant fire,
the no-man's land between us pitted
with mines that would cut you down years later
unless defused by a team of experts
clutching helmets, meters, odd vacuum cleaners.

As if such experts exist.
As if it were not too late
to deploy them.

Walking Underwater

Dana, Massachusetts: Town, 25 miles WNW of Worcester. Legally ceased to exist in 1938, when the Quabbin Reservoir was created. When the reservoir is full, almost half of the former township is underwater.

Wandering off the road to Dana, we two wade
through fields waist-deep in goldenrod,
with goldfinches crossing before us,
their flight rising & falling like waves.
Part of me listens to my friend.
Another part fingers feathery grasses
anchored in this broken road
as if I were blind, lost,
& asking the things around me for answers.

Lilies of the valley thrive in scrawled rows
beside cellar holes. Vestiges of hedges break ranks,
but the barberry's thorn still guards its scarlet fruit.
A wild turkey's ghostly gobbling echoes
like colonial war whoops through the woods.
A vulture waits on the horizon
without lifting a wing,
circling over a town already picked clean.

No—here's a baby snake, crushed by a logging truck.
I touch the heart-shaped leaves
of a bush whose name we do not know
as they bathe in the light
which this year means drought.

The road to the reservoir does not end
where it is supposed to plunge: past Dead Man's Curve.
We hike down among black, skull-like stumps
with roots & branches sticking up like antlers.

Twenty feet below the waterline, we
look over our shoulders at the beach.
This place feels like the aftermath of a disaster,
yet pondweed calmly flowers in powdery blue
where fish once swam, where hay once grew.
The road has been washed too clean—
Noah, stepping on land again,
surrounded by all that righteousness.

Were ribs of the drowned sinners underfoot?
Did the paired forebears of bubonic rats
scamper over them?

A modern plague has made my telephone a wound
that never stops hemorrhaging grim news.

My friend, my former science teacher, takes my picture.
She has her own problems, asks my advice, then
tells of contradictory theories which explain
how all the dinosaurs ran in the same direction
when they left their tracks along the riverbank.
I'm wondering what these dry weeds mean, & these
rusted pitons stuck like fossils in the mud, why we're able
to hike further than ever on this road
past stolen barnyards half-offered back
by some flip-flopping god

who now seems to want to reclaim the love
for one another that men just barely won
—the decade after Stonewall like a field
cleared rock by wearying rock—
by flooding our fields   *If I could only explain*
then drying them   *If I could only explain the cruelty*

    & then turning them into dust   *If I could only explain*
                      the cruelty of these relapses
     once another bout with pneumonia is won
        & then turning them into dust
              the wind will carry away.

Inside me, there once was a valley
behind this dam of cracking secrets
it took years to construct

            & then it over-
    flows Why why why
do the young sicken & fall before the old
& return in dreams of green childhood
where gardens stay lush & hailstones never fall,
dreams like islands that once were hills
& are hills again, but provide no vantage
in this nightmare where I'm walking underwater,
holding a phone that keeps ringing,
& have no teacher to tell me how
pondweed, left high & dry, knows to flower.

House Guest with AIDS

We put on a record to hear you sing.
Your lover lights up: he didn't know you back then.
Your pillbox alarm goes off again.
Every few hours, it recalls the end,
its blank white more recurrent than moonlight,
this ticking oblong in your pocket
that no one wants to talk about.

Dizzy, nauseous, oh so thin, you can't attend
to tonight's board game. Wordlessly
putting stemware away, we wonder
if you're still our guest, or have already left.
So this is death, this drift between here &
gone, gone & here. Days later
behind the haze you disappear.

The pokerfaced moon illuminates waving
power lines through a scrim of clouds.
Would that it witnessed us.
Half in darkness
or eclipsing our light,
like a ghost it reminds us
how much glides past our earthbound sight.

The Ferry of Your Dementia

Hollow cheeks, glittery eyes,
a tidemark of spittle and pill
crusting one corner
of your still-frequent sneer,
sometimes bedazzled smile.

Teeth clenched, you go for the burn!—
up an escalator where scoured
steel Metro absorbs the glare
above Virginia's sprawl.
You bark at a black girl
not standing to one side.
She doesn't lay into you,

but I do (unfairly?),
then: shaking, I
sign the line for new-
car smell. Rent
a thin smile. Jingle
both keys: *All aboard!*
Next stop: Harper's Ferry!
You stare ahead, lower the raw
toothpick you've become
onto the other front seat,
lift in one leg, then the other
as if stepping into a boat.

I shadow the Potomac
till it takes on Shenandoah as its own,
slices through Blue Ridge
where the Alleghenies herd us
along furrows, force highways to aim
where rivers must blend.

—Where crazy John Brown
should've thought ahead,
never let that train move on.

Between the dovetailed V
of a crumbling stone foundation,
the park rangers tell us to split
into two camps. You choose
to keep your seat on a stump
with the Confederates.
I fume with the Union,
suspect you're clear
about goading me,
or are you bone-
tired, just glad
for a sunlit breath
in the battle?

Back in the car, map
askew across sharp knees,
you squawk, *Turn right!*
I, helmsman adrift, wish for a sign
to a city we don't already know,
but of course I merge
into the left-turn lane,
towards naptime's thrown-up dosage,
swept between shaded banks
of the insistent River Styx.

Deathwatch

Your wan hallucinations
flicker on the ceiling:
rippled portents of
an aqua passage.
Mother & lover hover,
change the Chux
smeared with evidence
of your helplessness.
You no longer monitor how
eyes probe like catheters,
flutter then flare like votive flames,
come back from the hallway
carnation pink.
Your vigil has ended.
Dully your eyes stare,
& dully they shine,
hinting only of
spacious surrender,
faceless relief.

What Remains

if there were a way to reach you,
a language to learn: conjunctions,
a subjunctive, a formal & familiar you

if there were a rosary to shinny up,
a way to climb, decade by decade,
mystery by mystery, into the indigo sky

if there were a highway in your direction,
an odometer to gauge the distance between us
like a modern Bethlehem star

if my car radio could chance upon you
singing Streisand songs through the static

if I could sprout antennae,
fizz like a Geiger counter, be launched
like a satellite to track gamma rays
from the black star you may now be

if I could sled downhill on a bright
December afternoon & feel again
your mittened fingers clasping my waist
as we dodge bare oaks,
skid out across the lake—
if the lake were not black gloss,
those runner-scrapes like icy scars

if I could find the chink, simply
tap & hear the hollow
behind the fake door,
then stumble through the tunnel
out of this galactic silence,
into what remains of your light,
I promise you would find me there.

After the Appointment with the Photographer Is Made

you want to show him your whole life
by taking him on a ride

past the village which lost its factory to fire
the Catholic school
which wouldn't take you as a boy
You didn't have a Polish last name

Past rowhouses
tacked over with roofing shingles
One attic serves as Nadolski's studio
the only other photographer you've sat before
when you were school-age & perfect
in a collarless jacket, a tiny bowtie
with your brother & sister, the three of you
still together in this life

Then past the New Birth Christian Church
that dyed your best friend's mind
Past two of the few still-working mills
that belch billows of bleached air
down this threadbare valley

Past the other church & the bingo sign
where you were baptized   in the ghost town
that once boasted *two* five-and-dimes
where you did all your Christmas shopping
before the mall cut in

Then up a hill & past two stubborn farms
You want to tell him it used to be like this everywhere
point out how stone walls trace

the roll & sense of the land
as they hug the valley's sides
how boulders stand like consciences
in the middle of pastures

You want to explain
this knockabout farm belonged
to your fifth-grade teacher
the one with dark hairs above her lip
who was almost too big to get out of her chair
yet whose fluttering fingers
hovered over her blotter
& taught you how to knot a thread

You pass the duplex you were born in
You wonder if he is taking this all in

The Lakota feared a photographer
would steal their souls
under his black hood

You fear he'll capture one look on your face
but leave you shouldering this
panorama of overlapping snapshots

    You can't help yourself   turn your car
    under the granite archway
    into the cemetery
    your new center of gravity

    You squat down, brush sand from the stone
    as if wiping your brother's brow

    You say
    take my picture here

IV.

It is the law of my own voice I shall investigate.
—Frank O'Hara, "Homosexuality"

Weeds of Woe

At thirteen, I wanted the whole
lot of 'em knocked off:
mother, father, sister, brother.
A fatal crash would do:
four dodos with one stone.
They wouldn't know what hit 'em.
The sympathy cards this orphan would amass!
I'd promenade down St. Paul's center aisle
tragic as Jackie K.
How could school shrinks guess
this sissy would manage just fine?
They hadn't a clue I could cook
& had scrumptious curtains
circled in the Sears catalog—
deep-violet faux-velvet drapes
framing puffy lavender sheers.
Kraft macaroni-and-cheese would frequent my menu
with a smidge of sweet pickle mix on the side—
I'd run my tongue over the bumpy
cauliflower, bite through
soft pearl onions.
Tailored in black, I'd swoop about,
trap beneath my rake each leaf that dared to flit
past pinions of my imported Inverness cape
(I'd scurry home from junior high
for Barnabas Collins rebroadcasts,
fearing & praying he'd slip into my
bedroom at dusk, make me blood-slave.)

Maybe I'd snap up one of those rotting
three-story Victorians I'd coveted.
Then, I'd have my own turret,
cupola, balcony, widow's

walk—stages to pace nights away,
lofting a candle, suppressing a smile.
I'd invite neighbors to gossip
about my rambling nimbus—
I wouldn't host a tour of the Garden Club,
but I wouldn't pull my shades, either,
as I ogled undershorts in catalogs
& heaved prodigious sighs.
Miss Havisham would have nothing on me.

But when scythe did rend
the youngest of us five dodos,
sever: bloody feathers.
After: strewn twigs
of a ground bird's pilfered nest. Forever:
never never Camp.

Just Before

(addressing his own image as a child in a photograph)

You there, bespectacled already & only
in the second grade, no longer the dreamy-eyed
toddler with Maybelline lashes
who'd look through the camera or glance
quizzically off to the left. Adrift,
you felt it no longer mattered where you looked—
no one cares about odd little boys
who pretend they're grouse, build roadside nests,
wave their wings at neighbors while brooding
over a clutch of stones. It no longer mattered:
the sun's glint on your glasses hid your gaze,
which turned inward as you waited
for some Superman to see through your homeliness
once two front teeth had replenished your smile.
You half-gathered there was more to
completion. The fairy godmother furnished
Cinderella with more than a gown—
things were clearer with glasses, &
you didn't like what you saw: your fledgling
body like skin on a hanger,
your sissy recess ways reviled.
You didn't like that it mattered, it mattered—
you'd have to learn to be somebody else
for them, understudy them
throughout your downy years,
years of wishing
as snow melted inside your boots
that someone would wave a beaded wand
instead of a Polaroid at you &

bring into focus your beauty,
your still-blurry daydreams
    of what it was like
        with the Prince
            just before midnight.

Robert Goulet Is Dead!

With your demise, one
sure-fire aphrodisiac flickers

but never goes out.
Five years old, hips
jammed against the fabric front
of our cabinet-sized stereo, I slithered
to where hidden speakers buzzed beneath
holster me   bolster me   tingle of your baritone
coxswain & oarsman
deep & firm & strong.

"If ever I should leave you,"
even down the hall, I'd tent, hard-
wired eardrum to hardwired taint.

If I place this disc just so,
we'll move together again:
Morocco me   embargo me
beverage & gargle me
roll me up & cabbage me
stallion as I lather you

Have me on a platter, please,
if you fancy food. Just
thrust all through a low note.
I wait in marinade.
You sound the sure vibrato.
You growl the deep-down way. Your dying
father made you vow to use the gift Dieu gave.
Merci, Père, for handing 'Tit-Gars the key
that turns the bolt in me:
wire me   high note   *fire me*
Conduit of dream.

I'm a socket hoping to be plugged,
a glance waiting to be met,
weak-kneed, obvious—a dizzy, cheap drunk—
shish-kabob, meatballs
laid out on a buffet
ladle me   cradle me
If ever you should leave her
reflect & connect
me   me   me
look up my number
on any heavenly wall.

My Perfect Confession

Bless me, Father, for I have sinned.
This is my first confession....
The nuns had drilled us to begin

just so, then list our transgressions
—as if, in that dim closet, each soul could
enter into grace through just one rote expression.

They said—perhaps they misunderstood—
that this was our one chance
to wipe clean all sin staining childhood,

that Father Grady's sidelong glance
through that yellowed, linen screen
stood in for the burning bush, God's lance-

like, all-knowing glare. If God had already seen
what I had done to my dink at night, why
must I now report my secret use of Vaseline?

To whom could I turn to supply
the grown-up words for what we boys had done—
our tingling skin, our silken thighs?

At seven, I'd reached The Age of Reason.
In bed at night, those misdeeds I could wear in public
I'd unpack, unfold, smooth out one by one;

silently rehearse my handpicked
offenses; then re-pack them in piles
tidy as lies. At church, the velvet curtain hung thick

in my hand as I slipped into the box. The tile
floor was no different inside than out. I heard a tap.
A crack of light widened, revealing the profile

of our priest. There was no way out of this trap.
I lied to my Mom. I shot a spitball at our dog Tory.
Then came that pause between a bolt & its thunderclap.

Forallmysins, Iamverysorry.
I waited for God to strike me dead.
I crept to the altar, knelt before our glistening Mary.

I whispered my penance while Jesus' heart bled.
Wouldn't justice, like a second hand, be swift & exact?
No: even breathing slows down when one's full of dread.

At the heavy front door, sunlight pushed me back.
As if sprung from nightmare, I knew with a start
God would let me live, with my guilt intact.

White Diamonds

(perfume commercial)

High-stakes poker in a black and white resort.
Prequel: grand entrances. First: stacked
goddess flirts with attendant paparazzi;
next: Adonis disembarks down tarmac *escalier*.
Backdrop: oasis with its desert horizon. Swaying
palm fronds, billowing sheers that beckon
and hint at pharaoh-sized beds, baths, unguents,
fragrant cotton. Mythic tryst. White buck of a god's
unbuttoned, as yet unfingered, silk.

Save him. So you can have him.
The Isis in you intervenes.

Not so fast, Von Ryan,
you warn, in a carefully careless drawl
that veils its lurking growl. Reputation:
the fastest woman in the known world,
whose flames the Vatican's mouthpiece deigns to condemn.
News flash: unrepentant.

These have always brought me luck:
on the table you toss many-carat clip-ons.
Easy come, easy go. Cleopatra's pearl dissolved,
a wager cheap vinegar won by eating away.
What are gems or vows to a velvet purr—
what is luck when heaven blesses with savage cleavage,
double-rowed lashes framing amethyst eyes—
Go ahead, Marc Antony, throw the dice.

Kitty Carlisle Is Dead!

I'm lonely without her. I'm lonelier without
a pal at work to tell I'm lonely,
but no colleague who's also male
modeled his poise on hers, &
there's no sense scaring the probably
bi accountant
with the tizzy this news flash has wreaked.

He hugged the chill out of me one bleak morning
while we waited for the office
Sumatra to brew. I guessed our contact
through sweater vests meant more to him,
that he was more cubicle than I.
Sometimes he tells me about obscure
French novels. At least I've heard of
les écrivains who captivate him;
that's my cachet. I picture
his wife & him on facing love seats,
reciting passages back & forth.

With whom can I commune about Kitty's
fitted shoulders, taffeta, how lipstick shone
in black & white? She set standards for any
conversation necklace & neckline should have,
enunciating questions with the elocution
of the Miss Porter's alumna I half-wanted to be:
never flummoxed, always an exponent
of the virtues of fine fabric, good breeding.
I read about a Forth Worth boy
whose turning point arrived as he came
face to face with Cruella de Vil on screen.
Did the same milkweed seed drift across the nation
to sprout fluff inside both of us?

Are we lost twins, yin & yin, that boy & I?
Is he mourning Kitty, too?

What if I'd never found a fellow
odd fellow? Spent my life composing
baroque postcards from La-La Land
with no one to mail them to?
When no one was around,
I looked up one "H"
word in a dictionary
so I'd know what "I" I was:
a boy who practiced comportment
over Hamburger Helper. I'd pretend I was royalty
or a regal panelist on a game show
where, for every contestant who told truth,
two lied skillfully as they could
about being Eisenhower's barber
or an actor playing an ape.
This morning's *Dispatch* upped
caffeine's usual emotional ante:
obituaries don't fib about death.
I long to parade through modular pods,
interrogating in a genteel voice
control panels & the networked
printers they regulate,
Kitty Carlisle is dead! Aren't your settings
feeling a bit queer today, too?

Postcard from P-Town

How could I not write to you here?
Ramshackle floorboards, painted lullaby-blue,
creak underfoot. You'd notice plaster-soft wood,
hollowed treads, guess at olden layers of gloss.
Up on the second floor, we're making a nest,
striding across rooms & rooms of bumpy sky!
Walls: butter-yellow. Woodwork: clean white.
We've opened every window to its screen.
Bird-chirps & breeze swirl through our tree house.
One side peers over a bower of wisteria—
I am not making this up, dear!—
benches placed, dream-like, for *tête-à-têtes*,
while heavy-headed dahlias nod—& I must mention
a truck just rattled the length of town,
delivering something wanted. How could I not
wish you were here?

Hello Dolly

a painting by Steve Walker, acrylic on canvas

Two gay G.I. Joes in Speedos
shake hands in midair, small-scale
trapeze artists with identical abs,
placed in each other's space
by two colossal hands—one tanned, one fair—
the bulk of the life-sized
men's bodies kept offstage.

"Gay" because brunet Joe unabashedly
assesses the blond's crotch
while the less worldly one
scans the eyes of his new acquaintance
for an answer that might make him
cry.

Something bestows
light behind the blond.
Though his deltoids bulge just as prodigiously,
his suit gleams diaper-white.
He sits hammocked halfway back
within the uplifted
palm of the paler statuesque hand,
offered up as sacrifice or prize.

There's a hint of God's fingers
letting Adam's go—of a firmament
beyond this blackish-blue backdrop.

The brunet, thrust from shadow,
suspended upright as if standing,
his right thigh spread wide,

gets pushed forward like a decoy
or specimen or tool ready at hand,
looks primed for all that follows
when doll skin meets.

Ishmael's Afterthoughts

"But though the picture lies thus tranced..."
Moby Dick, Chapter One

I curl under our covers
after my considerate savage
tucked shut the door on his way downstairs.
Finally at ease, in spite of
this God-forsaken mattress
(*stuffed with seashells*, I joked to myself,
long after Queequeg snuffed out the light),
I absolutely must linger
to face bumpy facts.
Half asleep, I slide my palms
where sheeted lumps still hold
the warmth of his harpooner's frame.
His arm around me & the rise it caused
thrust the answer upon me.
No wonder I jostled, cajoled, roused him
so pointedly, repeatedly, insistently.
Of course I recoiled at first, aroused
by a heathen's unconscious clasp.
Who would simply embrace
a damned identity? But
a mind of my own I've always had,
working out facts to their logical ends.
Methinks my Creator blessed me with this curse.
When the needle of my compass
should be whizzing madly,
I have an anchor, an explanation
for the foul weather icing my soul,
even through April, when my best pupils
thought me God. The architecture
of sailors & their shoulders I ached for unawares,

their massive calves scaling mizzenmasts,
their horsepower torsos sprawled at sunset,
their swearing & snoring & silence—
for these I blackened my name,
walked away from my post
before term's end.

I should have nuzzled, but barely,
against his tattoos at daybreak,
mapped my Pacific paradise.

Like a whale that must sometimes breach, or die,
might this pagan roll beside me
if invited by my eyes? Might there be a signal—
might there be a softness—
might two Polynesian paddlers
sway together in rituals
unimagined by preachers?

And if the same whaler took us both on
to yearn three years
        across hammocks?

                Up with me!—
to breakfast, to my bunk-mate's side,
where he points his boots
toward the docks, a destiny without.
There are forbidden things
a quiet man may quietly desire.
I couldn't yet embrace the dream
embracing me at dawn,
but given one more chance, for all the world
I wouldn't break that waking's sacred trance.

Walking behind Tennyson at Cauteretz

Henry Graham Dakyns, 1861

All along the valley I stall ten yards behind,
not wishing to distract a grief much rawer still than mine.
All along the valley I will not blurt, *I knew.*
I will not try your confidence. I will not breathe, *Me, too.*

Since Hallam never fancied your frank grin as you hoped
(pale hip glowing milkily; bedsheet lifted, mute),
all along this valley, undress before *What then?*

(Ahhh…
Many a coal sighs low, no tinder tempting blaze.)

Never a deeper sorrow could anchor in your soul,
never another unkissed mouth unnestle all you fold.
Never another donkey ride to ponder what you shared
alongside what you didn't, because your sister did.

Never before you die will you be followed by such as me
who fingers clues of avalanche on every stone and tree.
All along the valley I hear you mumble low,
but let you rein, reverse, converse with echoes long ago.
All along the valley, bloom and stem pressed tight,
I tuck my gift inside my book—don't trouble thee with sight.

V.

Surely all art is the result of one's having been in danger, of having gone through an experience all the way to the end.
—Carolyn Forché, "The Angel of History"

Cyndi Lauper

From the first bash of drums,
    we can bet this won't be pretty.
She's *dialing up 911*—
    in a stomp-squeal frenzy of escape,
a wail all lisp & ache, its silver spike
    heels nearly skewering comic-book scraps,
untied ribbons underfoot.

    A soul's entrails. Road-kill of an ecstasy
that never looked both ways.
    Skipped drumbeats ricochet
down the block. An empty lot.
    Her siren's stiletto
stab-stitches the sky.
    A house of cards
props up one final offer
    till our blond stops holding her
breath.

    Girl-wire whose plea
scrapes down to grieving
    baby talk. The beauty is we know
what she's groaning about.

Hearth Hold

The brew boils over, makes my fire die;
The wind huffs till it croaks
To bring to leaf again the log my big heart pokes.
—Jules LaForgue, "Complaint de l'automne monotone"

Perhaps the brew was hexed, malevolent,
launching vengeance versus fire,
that age-old plague of plants.
Perhaps this boiling-over began an epoch
when vegetables, in agony, rose up,
even those plucked, chopped,
ground between pestle and mortar—
broth of stalk, seed, and leaf swelling up
to save a captive log by swamping fire.

Wind has its own way, whistles past
open drafts, confounds kindling
before dry heat takes hold,
before stoking becomes possible.
Breeze knows bark to quicken,
remembers how spring leaves rustle
(tender tips of sprigs uplifting),
guesses at root hair thrust
through ash, whispers *Tree*
to what's split open.

Does anything simply burn here?
Did this blaze provoke its dousing
when it licked the pot too hard?
Was the parsnip innocent,
a root incapable of rage?
How could it be possible

to cease watching over sparks
when we portage conflagration,
keeping matches wrapped aloft;

and how could heart not beat here,
having suffered all the roles:
though scalded, stripped of bark,
or stuffed and swiveled on a spit,
now hoping for a gale, what remedy does it know
but to nudge, nudge the smoking log
that blazes back and snaps?

Ophelia Approaches

i.

His feigned beclouded mind
became her whimsical rhyme.
When his thrust pierced that arras
and her father's side,
it breached her parapet.
The nunnery she waded in
proved a whirlpool whose babbling
dragged her down. Out of
another's tragedy swirled her own.

ii. September 2005

Wind chimes shudder, jangled
by the eyelash of the storm.
Already brittle leaves rattle against bark,
buffeted by what squalls remain.
Flocked grackles huddle, exeunt
ahead of gusts, these leftover
huffs from the Sahara's slingshot
sprung off a continent's steam, these
wisps of someone else's suffering,
something amiss in our sphere.

With Nothing New

oarsmen from aged ships   pried
then jailed in carts of swiftly hewn   bars
guarded by   cudgels
and still these naked captives rise in song   thrust
jaws against splintered   bark
with all their might   gore
streaked torsos heaving out   clots
of buzz and drone   swelling
over the clatter of rim on   gravel
galloping toward a milder coast's   manacles

gagged, cuffed, blindfolded   coxswain
hunched, vomit-drenched, in shock   slave
concludes   *Now I must learn from this*
blackness   *to steer without rudder, without*
commands   *without cat-o'-nine-tails, the I who*
flogged   *then starved them into bleating, the I who*
shoved   *their great spent limbs into "the hole" —with*
nothing   *I must lead them to an early*
death   *our inlets could swaddle with song*

Swimming the Contoocook

June 2006

Boys play at paratroopers
plunge one   two   three   four
off the covered bridge   So far the drop
the angle of their limbs   crucial
as they knife through midstream
We tsk at their sense of safety

One   two   middle-aged men
we pad our flip-flops
down a pea-stone path
to barely a beach
strip down to Speedos
another kind of risk

Main Street traces riverbank
and lining sidewalks today   countless flags
some stuck into lawns like pinwheels
some stapled   some hanging from fists
as the hearse slides by
Corners of bigger flags twined into chain link
along the overpass   where Magic-Markered top sheets
flap   "Thank you, Russell, for protecting our town"

The boys sprint to where knotted rope
swings out from a branch
of a half-gone tree   its furthest reach
a third of this river's span
I think   *Boulder*   They think   *Blast*
They guffaw   yelp   soar out in twos
"You kicked me in the balls!" one pipes

We who have daily guided razors
round corners of mouths
tiptoe past poison ivy to the spot
to slip in   You've volunteered
as lifeguard   and watch for bubbles
from snapping turtles

You've a baritone I could back-flip into
its New York burble smooth enough
if you weren't straight   if I weren't married
if we weren't actuaries
of the granite beneath

In the runnel of sky unfurling
above the seam of this valley hamlet
above our backstroking hands
up where next week's fireworks will embroider the dark
Someone turned on the Military Channel
"Military ER" the show
Tweezers grapple shrapnel
from a torso in Iraq
      I avert my mind's eye back
      to the glistening meadow beyond tall oaks
      to the roof of the Victorian library
      where mourners cling beside their cars
but blood keeps drawing my focus skyward
to the grunt's trusting eyes
I wonder where the remote is
who picked this channel

Abandoning the backstroke we strain toward the bridge
Kicking against the current as it ripples mid-river
I mark one tree to make sure I am moving
Our talk falls off for the effort

And finally we feel the luxury
of letting ourselves be carried back
towards boys   rope   all we grappled with
through summer camp's gashes
stitches   interrogations   before
we could become these two men
paddling together   and maybe
we'll help each other clamber up the steep
or offer a hand   at least

When we're done drying off
though constantly now
that soldier's childlike gaze posters my sky
I hesitate to ask
When you studied lifesaving
did they cover not just whitewater but dark
how to prop dead weight above the surface
how to talk about skulls
with boys who can fly

Backward Glance

*Block V, South Frieze, Parthenon Sculptures,
British Museum*

Smooth-faced backward glance
surfaces from swirling stream
of uncarved marble. Boy-man
thrust into clatter of battle,
his steed's mane and his own
forelocks flattened by the gale
grim galloping whips up. How much horse
has crumbled off this block,
or was it left unhewn?
Torso of fresh muscles
our only other chiseled glimpse
of this buck's being dashed
towards blade's-edge, now he has spurred.
What fear springs from his limestone eye!—
as he peers back above a blond cheek
with no time to ponder
his mother's folded sorrow
when his slingshot stunned a sparrow,
or to hover like a floating ghost
over a tutored lesson's tablet
where he'd etched *Thermopylae* in wax—
a reckless scrying over his shoulder
as he hears what rattles right behind:
the choice to be trampled
or speared from the rear
or to hurtle into his own beheading.
No nightmare could have schooled him how
cold a stone can grow, how unfinished it can last.

Notes

W.S. Merwin translated the lines quoted from Canto XI of Dante's *Purgatorio*.

"Upon Reading Tennessee Williams' Obituaries": the italicized quotations are from his *Memoirs* (New York: Bantam Books, 1976); his *Notebooks* (New Haven: Yale University Press, 2006); his "A Separate Poem," from *In the Winter of Cities* (New York: New Directions, 1964); Donald Windham (editor), *Tennessee Williams' Letters to Donald Windham 1940-1965* (Harmondsworth: Penguin Books, 1977); and Lyle Leverich, *Tom: The Unknown Tennessee Williams* (New York: Crown Publishers, 1995).

"House Guest with AIDS" is in memory of Kenny Arkin (1955-1990).

"What Remains": Each group of ten rosary beads is called a decade. A traditional way to say the rosary is to concentrate on one of the fifteen Holy Mysteries (based largely on scenes from the life of Jesus Christ) while reciting a particular number of prayers.

"After the Appointment with the Photographer Is Made" is for the photographer Robert Giard, who died in 2002.

"Robert Goulet Is Dead!": "'Tit-Gars" is a Franco-American nickname meaning "Little Guy."

"My Perfect Confession" is for Charlotte Grace. The possibility of a "perfect" or complete confession has been debated over centuries within the Roman Catholic Church.

"Kitty Carlisle Is Dead!" is for Martha E. Stone. The English translation of "*les écrivains*" is "the writers."

"Postcard from P-town" is for Charles F. Gustina.

"Hearth Hold": Peter Dale translated the epigraph quoted from LaForgue.

Acknowledgements

Grateful acknowledgement is made to the editors of the following journals and anthologies, in which earlier versions of these poems appeared:

Assaracus: "Crayola Cruella," "Hello Dolly," "Lena Horne," "Lost Soul," "Postcard from P-town," "Robert Goulet Is Dead!," "Sighted during a Whale Watch," "The Teacup I Desire," "Walking behind Tennyson at Cauteretz," "Weeds of Woe," "White Diamonds"

Bay Windows: "House Guest with AIDS"

Christopher Street: "Walking Underwater"

Evergreen Chronicles: "After the Appointment with the Photographer Is Made," "Just Before," "What Remains"

Le Forum: "Meditations on Yellow," "With Nothing New"

Gay & Lesbian Review: "Deathwatch"

International Poetry Review: "Hearth Hold"

Journal of Gay, Lesbian, and Bisexual Identity: "My Perfect Confession"

OVS Magazine: "Chris Evert"

Peregrine: "Blackberrying," "Cyndi Lauper"

Poetry Porch: "Backward Glance," "Kitty Carlisle Is Dead!"

RFD: "My Invisible Dress"

SNReview: "Fingernails," "For Patrick, My New Nurse"

Tygerburning Literary Review: "Swimming the Contoocook"

"My Perfect Confession" also appeared in *Collective Brightness: LGBTIQ Poets on Faith, Religion & Spirituality* (Sibling Rivalry Press).

"Chris Evert" also appeared in *Divining Divas: 100 Gay Men on Their Muses* (Lethe Press)

"White Diamonds" also appeared in *Rabbit Ears: TV Poems* (Poets Wear Prada).

I would like to express heartfelt thanks to many teachers, editors, fellow students and workshop members, and friends for giving me feedback and guidance. I am most especially indebted to Michael Waters, Joan Larkin, Carol Frost, Tayve Neese, Roberta Feins, Lisa Sisler, Terry Lucas, Paula McClain, and Ira Sadoff from the New England College MFA in Poetry Program; John Drury at the Antioch Writers' Workshop; Kevin McLellan at the Cambridge Center for Adult Education; Pat Schneider and Patricia Lee Lewis from Amherst Writers & Artists; the late Roland Flint at Georgetown University; Julia Lisella at the Harvard Extension School; Elizabeth Robinson at the Iowa Writers' Workshop; and Christopher Bursk, Edison Dupree, David Eberly, Randi Schalet, Geoff Wisner, and Robin Becker. As always, my husband Neil Glickman deserves my deepest gratitude.

About the Author

Steven Riel is the author of three chapbooks of poetry: *How to Dream*, *The Spirit Can Crest*, and most recently, *Postcard from P-town*, which was selected as runner-up for the inaugural Robin Becker Chapbook Prize and published in 2009 by Seven Kitchens Press. His poems have appeared in several anthologies and in numerous periodicals, including *The Minnesota Review, International Poetry Review, Evening Street Review, Christopher Street, The G.W. Review, St. Andrew's Review, The James White Review, and The Antigonish Review*. In 2005, Christopher Bursk named him the Robert Fraser Distinguished Visiting Poet at Bucks County (PA) Community College. He served as poetry editor of *RFD* between 1987 and 1995. He won a grant from the Massachusetts Cultural Council in 1992. His poems were nominated for the Pushcart Prize in 1989 and for *Editors' Choices III* in 1991. He holds both an MFA in Poetry and an MLS and works as Manager of Serials Cataloging at Harvard University Library.

About the Artist

Jim Jackson is a multi-media artist and designer who has lived and worked for many years in Cambridge, MA, but now spends most of his days in his studio in Vermont. He was born in Arkansas and raised in Texas where he earned a BFA from the University of Texas with many awards and scholarships.

Jim was awarded two National Endowment grants for travel and study which he used to earn an MFA from Pratt Institute. In NYC he spent time as an art and education consultant for the Metropolitan Museum and Parks Department.

He has shown widely in Texas, New York, Massachusetts and Vermont; wrote and illustrated *Seeing Yourself See;* and founded a company that produces anatomy and biological models.

website: www.jimjacksonart.com

About the Book

Fellow Odd Fellow was designed at Trio House Press through the collaboration of:

Tayve Neese, Lead Editor
Jim Jackson, Cover Art: *Dancing Green & Orange*
Dorinda Wegener, Cover Design
Lea Deschenes, Interior Design

The text is set in Adobe Caslon Pro.

The publication of this book is made possible, whole or in part, by the generous support of the following individuals and/or agencies:

Anonymous

About the Press

Trio House Press is a collective press. Individuals within our organization come together and are motivated by the primary shared goal of publishing distinct American voices in poetry. All THP published poets must agree to serve as Collective Members of the Trio House Press for twenty-four months after publication in order to assist with the press and bringing more Trio books into print. Award winners and published poets must serve on one of four committees: Production and Design, Distribution and Sales, Educational Development, or Fundraising and Marketing. Our Collective Members reside in cities from New York to San Francisco.

Trio House Press adheres to and supports all ethical standards and guidelines outlined by the CLMP.

Trio House Press, Inc. is dedicated to the promotion of poetry as literary art, which enhances the human experience and its culture. We contribute in an innovative and distinct way to American Poetry by publishing emerging and established poets, providing educational materials, and fostering the artistic process of writing poetry. For further information, or to consider making a donation to Trio House Press, please visit us online at: www.triohousepress.org.

Other Trio House Press Books you might enjoy:

Flight of August by Lawrence Eby
    2013 Louse Bogan Winner selected by Joan Houlihan

The Consolations by John W. Evans
    2013 Trio Award Winner selected by Mihaela Moscaliuc

The Ghosts of Lost Animals by Michelle Bonczeck Evory, 2013

Clay by David Groff
    2012 Louse Bogan Winner selected by Michael Waters

Gold Passage by Iris Jamahl Dunkle
    2012 Trio Award Winner selected by Ross Gay

If You're Lucky Is a Theory of Mine by Matt Mauch, 2012

www.ingramcontent.com/pod-product-compliance
Lightning Source LLC
Chambersburg PA
CBHW030604020526
44112CB00048B/1209